D0849282

DESMOND TUTU

by David Winner

Picture credits
Associated Press, p. 4; Omar Badsha, p. 46; BBC Hulton Picture Library: Mal Langsdon, p. 45 (top left); Camera Press: Jacob Sutton, p. 30; Fair Lady, p. 54 (both); International Defence and Aid Fund for Southern Africa, pp. 8, 9 (both), 10, 12, 15 (both), 17, 22, 23, 26, 28, 35, 36 (top), 47 (below), 50-51, 52, 57; Link: Jillian Edelstein, pp. 42, 47 (top); Orde Eliason, pp. 29, 33, 38, 42 (top right and bottom left), 59 (top); Greg English, pp. 36, 40, 49; Peter Magubane, p. 34; Monitor, cover; Photo Source: C. Friend, p. 7; Popperfoto, pp. 16, 21; Reuters: Wendy Schwegmann, p. 53; Reflex: Philip Littleton, p. 59 (below); Rex Features, p. 37; Rogan Coles, p. 44; Durand, pp. 11, 58 (top); Gunston, p. 51 (above); J. Kuus, p. 58 (below); Frank Spooner: J. Chiasson, p. 51 (below); Chips Hire, p. 45 (below right); Desmond Tutu, pp. 19, 31; U.S.P.G.: Bryan Heseltine, p. 6.

Maps drawn by Geoffrey Pleasance

To Caroline

Exley Publications would like to thank Desmond Tutu for allowing us to reproduce personal photographs in this book. We would also like to give special thanks to Mr. John Allen, Mrs. Crawford-Browne, and other members of the Archbishop's Office for their advice and cooperation. We are most grateful to Shirley du Boulay, author of *Tutu: Voice of the Voiceless*, for generously sharing her research material, and to Wendy Coleman and Shirley Moulers, who gave us great help with our research.

North American edition first published in 1989 by
Gareth Stevens, Inc.
7317 West Green Tree Road
Milwaukee, WI 53223 USA

First published in the United Kingdom in 1989 with an
original text © 1989 by Exley Publications Ltd.
Additional end matter © 1989 by Gareth Stevens, Inc.

Library of Congress Cataloging-in-Publication Data

Winner, David, 1956-
    Desmond Tutu.

    (People who have helped the world)
    Includes index.
    Summary: Examines the life of the South African bishop and civil rights worker who
has worked extensively to improve the condition of his people.
    1. Tutu, Desmond. 2. Church of the Province of South Africa--Bishops--Biography.
3. Anglican Communion--South Africa--Bishops--Biography. [1. Tutu, Desmond. 2. Civil
rights workers. 3. Clergy. 4. Blacks--Biography. 5. South Africa--Race relations] I.
Title. II. Series.
BX5700.6.Z8T878   1988   283'.092'4 [B] [92]   88-4883
ISBN 1-55532-847-4
ISBN 1-55532-822-9 (lib. bdg.)

Series conceived and edited by Helen Exley
Picture research: Kate Duffy
Research: Diana Briscoe
Editorial: Margaret Montgomery
Series editor, U.S.: Rhoda Irene Sherwood
Editor, U.S.: Kelli Peduzzi
Editorial assistant, U.S.: Scott Enk

Printed in Hungary

1 2 3 4 5 6 7 8 9 94 93 92 91 90 89

DESMOND TUTU

The courageous and eloquent Archbishop struggling against apartheid in South Africa

by David Winner

Gareth Stevens Publishing
Milwaukee

Protest in Cape Town

Even for the toughest campaigners against South Africa's cruel system of apartheid, the news of February 24, 1988, came as a shock.

Over the years, the government run by Whites had systematically crushed all opposition by Blacks.* Now the United Democratic Front, a nonracial group, and sixteen other organizations were also silenced, and their leaders arrested. It was brutally clear that South Africa's white leaders wouldn't let *anyone* oppose them, even when the protesters were members of many racial groups and completely nonviolent.

With all other black and anti-apartheid political leaders banned, in jail, or in exile, the churches were now the only organizations powerful enough to challenge the government openly. Archbishop Desmond Tutu, the most respected, prominent, and outspoken of all the church leaders, was one of the very few black leaders left who could lead the fight for justice.

He called the major religious leaders of the country together in his cathedral in Cape Town to protest the law. They met on February 29, 1988. Archbishops, priests, and ministers of almost every Christian denomination in South Africa gathered at the cathedral. First they prayed together. Then they linked arms and marched out of the cathedral to the government headquarters a few hundred yards away.

*To oppose their government's system of classifying people according to color and to express their solidarity with Blacks, many South Africans that the South African government refers to as "Coloureds" and "Asians" now call themselves Black. In this text, however, "Blacks" refers to native Africans.

"The government's idea of reform is to smash all political opposition in the country, no matter how peaceful and lawful, and to rule with the jackboot."
Desmond Tutu, after the February 24, 1988, decree

"[We are not] the usual bunch of rabble-rousers."
Desmond Tutu, at a news conference of clergymen defending the Church's right to protest apartheid

Archbishop Desmond Tutu (middle) marches peacefully toward the police lines in Cape Town to protest the government's banning of opposition groups. With him are the other religious leaders, now the only remaining legal voice of opposition to apartheid. On the left is Allan Boesak; on the right is Archbishop Stephen Naidoo. All were briefly arrested for this protest.

5

Many of South Africa's twenty-one million Blacks are forced by the white government to live in crowded conditions without electricity, running water, or sewers. The racist law of apartheid virtually guarantees poverty among Blacks. In the rich, beautiful land of South Africa, Blacks have no political or economic say in their own futures.

The goal of this group was to hand a petition to the prime minister. But as they approached the government headquarters, a line of heavily armed riot police blocked their way. As the religious leaders neared the line, a policeman ordered them to disperse.

The marchers refused. Then they kneeled at the policemen's feet. For a moment, the police seemed not to know what to do. They seemed confused and uncertain about arresting members of the clergy. Then an order was given. Policemen roughly dragged Archbishop Tutu and the others away. They were under arrest.

Tutu was one of the best known church leaders in the world and the police dared not keep the religious men locked up for too long. Tutu's companions, including Allan Boesak, leader of the World Alliance of Reformed Churches, were almost equally well known and respected. But as far as the country's government was concerned, this peaceful protest amounted to nothing more than troublemaking.

For more than forty years, the white rulers of South Africa had tried to crush the country's Blacks into submission by passing laws against them, although they had owned land and lived in the country for centuries before white people had even arrived. While many Whites had servants and houses with swimming pools, most Blacks lived in desperate poverty without electricity, water, or toilets. These and many other injustices were the result of the laws of apartheid.

As a result of the law, black fathers were forced to spend eleven months of the year at hard labor away from their wives and children, who often went hungry.

As a result of the law, thousands of black people had to get up at three o'clock in the morning to travel long distances to work each day because they weren't allowed to live in the cities.

As a result of the law, Blacks could not vote. Even though there were five times as many black people as white, Blacks had no say in who governed them.

As a result of the law, black families who had lived in their homes for generations were moved out and dumped in barren, desolate places hundreds of miles away on the orders of any white official.

Anyone who protested these or other injustices could be beaten or put in prison. That was also a result of the law.

Now the government was preventing people from even peacefully trying to change the law. "What is it," asked Boesak, "that the South African government wants the people to do?"

On the other side of the racial divide, many of South Africa's four-and-a-half million Whites live in surroundings like those shown here in Stellenbosch. White homes have running water, electricity, and trash collection.

The first Whites

The roots of the confrontation that day in Cape Town went deep into history.

Discrimination by white people against black people in South Africa had been going on ever since white settlers arrived in the country nearly 350 years earlier — ironically, at almost exactly the spot where Archbishop Tutu made his protest.

The first Europeans to live in South Africa were Dutch. In 1652, they set up a permanent settlement at

Black servitude under Whites began hundreds of years ago. This picture depicting seventeenth-century South Africa shows black workers being supervised by white settlers in the early days of the Cape Colony.

"That has been the political history of South Africa: how Whites could maintain their position of privilege, based on the biological accident and irrelevancy of the color of their skins."

Desmond Tutu,
in Hope and Suffering

the Cape, the very tip of Africa. Ships of the powerful Dutch East India Company would stop there for fresh food, water, and fuel. The Dutch merchants and sailors enjoyed relaxing there in the pleasant climate.

At that time, the huge land that is now called South Africa was inhabited by African peoples such as the Xhosa, Ndebele, Sotho, Tswana, and Zulu. The unfortunate people who lived nearest the new white settlers were two ancient, gentle, nomadic peoples: the San and the Khoikhoi, whose traditional way of life had existed for thousands of years.

Tragically for them, the Cape soon became an important stopping place for more white people.

At first the new arrivals from Europe got along well with the local people, but the peace did not last long. The settlers wanted local cattle and sheep for food. In the early days, they bought these animals from Africans. As the Cape settlement grew, they stole them. The Khoikhoi fought back with spears, bows, and arrows, but their resistance was doomed. The guns of the Whites were too powerful. Tens of thousands of

Khoikhoi were killed in battle. Thousands more died of infections brought by the settlers.

In the years that followed, boatloads of white settlers from Germany, France, and the Netherlands gradually conquered the Blacks native to the area. The Europeans settled the land all around. The Cape became a colony of Europe, hundreds of square miles in size. Most of the incoming people were farmers. They became known as Boers. Over the years, the several languages they spoke evolved into one new language called Afrikaans, and many Afrikaans-speaking Boers became prosperous.

But the Cape was becoming a place of great suffering for native Africans. The few surviving Khoikhoi had to do menial jobs. The Boers treated them much like slaves. In addition, the Boers brought thousands of black slaves from other parts of Africa to the colony to work for them. Living conditions were terrible. Life was cruel and inhuman for the black Africans. Slaves or workers who tried to run away were savagely punished or even killed.

This pattern of white conquest and black suffering was to become a way of life in South Africa. It was going to make South Africa's history a tragic history. One day the world would turn its eyes to South Africa and would not like what it saw.

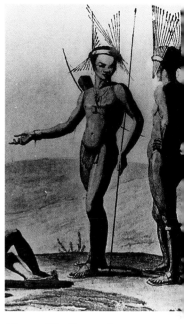

Above: The San and Khoikhoi peoples suffered at the hands of early settlers. Below: Boers drive the Xhosa over the Fish River in the Wars of Dispossession in the1780s.

*During the Great Trek,
Boer settlers, called
"Voortrekkers," fought off
attacking Zulu in the
Battle of Vegkop. The
Zulu armies fought
bravely, but their spears
and shields were no match
for the Boers' rifles. The
Boers ultimately carved
out their own republics by
conquering all the tribes
and land in the South
African interior.*

The British take over

In 1814, the wars against Napoleon ended. One result of the wars was that Britain took over the Cape Colony from the Dutch. They then ruled both the Boers and the Africans.

The British were as racist as the Dutch. They, too, did not consider the black people their equals. They had, however, abolished the slave trade, and were moving to abolish slavery throughout the rest of the British Empire. But it took them until 1833, nearly twenty years after they had taken over the Cape Colony, to demand that the Boers free their slaves.

The Boers resented this. They had gotten used to years of white supremacy over the native Africans. Some of them had even been known to shoot San people for sport. They thought the British were arrogant, and they resented British rule in the first place. So when the British demanded that they free their slaves, they were furious at what they saw as a restriction of their *own* freedom! They began to protest the overbearing attitude and laws of the British.

The "Great Trek"

Boer protests against the antislavery laws had no effect. So many of them decided to leave and set up their own countries, or republics, far away to the north and east of the Cape. From 1835 until the 1840s, between six thousand and fourteen thousand Boers set off in wagons on their journey.

Today, Afrikaans speakers (or Afrikaners) still think of this, and other expeditions which followed, as a heroic exploit called the "Great Trek" and are proud of their ancestors, the *Voortrekkers*, who made them.

The Voortrekkers may have thought they were heading off to an empty land, but they were really carrying out an invasion. In the years that followed, they clashed with African armies who were sent to defend their lands against the invaders. The most powerful were the Zulus, who had themselves only recently conquered much of southern Africa. But even the much-feared Zulu spears and *impis,* or battalions, were no match for the modern Boer rifles and cannons, and in 1838 the Zulus were finally defeated.

Eventually, the Boers succeeded in carving out two new republics for themselves: the Orange Free State and Transvaal. Many black people there were put to work on land which had once been their own.

Gold and diamonds

In the 1870s, the biggest reserve of diamonds ever found was discovered at Kimberley.

As soon as the British realized how much money could be made out of this discovery, they decided to grab the diamond fields for themselves. In the next few years they swiftly conquered most of the remaining African kingdoms in the country and recruited thousands of black men to work in the new diamond mines. These men were treated like prisoners.

At that time, of course, most Europeans did not see very much wrong with this way of doing things. In the name of "civilization," Europeans were still busily colonizing countries all over the world to add to their empires, and no one was doing so more eagerly than the British. At best, conquered peoples could expect to be treated with disdain. At worst, they were treated

"History, like beauty, depends largely on the beholder so when you read that, for example, David Livingstone discovered the Victoria Falls, you might be forgiven for thinking that there was nobody around the Falls until Livingstone arrived on the scene."

Desmond Tutu, on the twentieth anniversary of the South African Republic

Afrikaners are proud of the Treks, which they celebrate each December 16. They dress up in Voortrekker clothes to celebrate their decisive defeat of the Zulu at the Battle of Blood River in 1838.

Diamond mines at Kimberley in the 1870s. The discovery of diamonds and gold brought great wealth to Whites but only suffering to the Blacks who worked in the mines. Note how the artist has depicted the cruelty of the overseer at left.

with great cruelty. Unfortunately for the conquered, the age when Europeans thought all people should be treated as equals was still a very long way off.

Soon an even more important discovery was made in South Africa. Vast gold fields were found in the Transvaal. Stretching for three hundred square miles, they formed the largest single concentration of gold yet known in the world.

British colonists flocked to the gold fields hoping to make their fortunes. This soon led to conflict with the Afrikaner republics over who would control the gold mines and the wealth. In 1899, these clashes became a full-scale war between the Afrikaners and the British Empire, known as the Boer War.

The Boer War was bitterly fought between the two

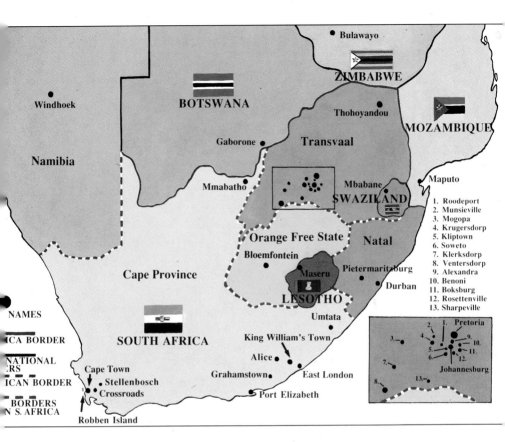

Windhoek

Namibia

BOTSWANA

Gaborone

Mmabatho

Cape Province

SOUTH AFRICA

Cape Town
Stellenbosch
Crossroads

Robben Island

Bulawayo

ZIMBABWE

Thohoyandou

MOZAMBIQUE

Transvaal

Mbabane

SWAZILAND

Maputo

Orange Free State

Bloemfontein

Maseru

LESOTHO

Umtata

King William's Town

Alice

Grahamstown

Port Elizabeth

East London

Natal

Pietermaritzburg

Durban

1. Roodeport
2. Munsieville
3. Mogopa
4. Krugersdorp
5. Kliptown
6. Soweto
7. Klerksdorp
8. Ventersdorp
9. Alexandra
10. Benoni
11. Boksburg
12. Rosettenville
13. Sharpeville

1. Pretoria
9.
10.
11.
12.
Johannesburg

white peoples in the country and lasted for three years. The Boers suffered huge losses. More than twenty thousand of their women and children died in British concentration camps. Eventually the Boers were defeated by the determined British.

Many thousands of Blacks, forced to fight on both sides, also died, but history books hardly mention their part in the war.

South Africa and the surrounding countries, showing the important places in Desmond Tutu's life. In 1987, Tutu would become Archbishop of South Africa, as well as of Lesotho, Namibia, Swaziland, and Mozambique.

New hardships

South Africa had finally been united by force of arms, and with the passing of the South Africa Act in 1910, it was given a new name: the Union of South Africa.

Defeated Afrikaners and the victorious British now made peace with each other. To help the peace process, the British gave the Afrikaners a large say in how the new country was run. That just made life

13

worse for South Africa's black people, whom Whites insultingly called *kaffirs*.

For decades, Blacks had been segregated from Whites. Now many laws discriminating against Blacks were passed by Afrikaner and English alike. Laws and policies like the poll tax forced Blacks to work for Whites in order to earn money to pay the tax. Other laws restricted where Blacks could work and even where they could live.

Whites, who made up only about a fifth of the whole population, took most of the country for themselves, including the best land. The few Blacks, Indians, and so-called "Coloureds"* who had been given the vote in the Cape had it taken away from them. Even marriages between Blacks and Whites became illegal.

Young Desmond

This was the world into which Desmond Mpilo Tutu was born on October 7, 1931, in Klerksdorp, a poor black township near Johannesburg, the richest city in South Africa.

Desmond Tutu's family was like the families of millions of other black South Africans. They did not have much money. Their home was small and crowded, and there was no electricity or sanitation. Their water came from a communal tap in the dry, dusty street.

The Tutus were subject to the same restrictions that affected all black people. Even though Desmond's father, Zachariah Tutu, was a respected schoolteacher, he had to carry a passbook, or special identification, like all other black people. White police would sometimes stop him on the street and demand his papers. This upset young Desmond because it seemed very unfair to him.

Although the Tutu family was poor, it was usually happy and loving. Their house was always full of visitors. Desmond's mother, Aletha Tutu, worked as a domestic servant to a white family. She was so kind and gentle that she was better known as *Komotso*, which means "comforter of the afflicted." Desmond also got along well with his three sisters, one of whom died when she was very young.

*See note on page 5.

Above: A desolate street scene in a typical black township.
Left: A family with no running water must make do with a tin bath outside.

This is the world into which Desmond Tutu was born: his bedroom was also the family dining and living room. He remarks that when young, he was a "township urchin" who went barefoot to school.

Father Trevor Huddleston (shown below in 1957) tirelessly campaigns against apartheid. He has inspired and has been a lifelong friend to Tutu. Father Trevor became an archbishop and president of the Anti-Apartheid Movement in Britain.

Zachariah and Aletha couldn't afford to buy Desmond many toys, but he and his friends found other ways to have fun. They played soccer with old tennis balls. They made model cars out of odds and ends. They took on small jobs. To make some money, Desmond sometimes sold oranges or was a caddy at a white golf club. Later, thinking of these years, Tutu described himself as a barefoot "urchin."

He was smart and worked hard at school, but he didn't yet show the saintly qualities for which he was later to become so famous. In fact, he could be mischievous. When he was about fourteen, he and a friend who rode fifteen miles by train to Western High School in Sophiatown became experts at cheating other passengers at cards. It's possible the workers were not fooled. It seemed they actually enjoyed the fun and nicknamed Desmond "the Professor." These exploits earned Tutu a little extra pocket money.

Like other young Blacks, Desmond always felt proud when he heard stories about successful Blacks in other countries. He was thrilled by the music of famous black American musicians like Louis Armstrong, and by the exploits of famous black athletes like the great Jesse Owens, the runner who won four gold medals in the 1936 Olympics.

And in his childhood, Tutu saw that not all Whites were cruel. One day he was out walking with his mother when they passed a tall white priest. To Desmond's amazement, the priest did something that was unheard of for a white man in South Africa. He smiled warmly at Mrs. Tutu and politely raised his hat. The priest was Father Trevor Huddleston, a man who would later have a great influence on Desmond's life.

When he was fourteen, Desmond caught tuberculosis and became dangerously ill. He lay in bed in a hospital full of dying men for nearly two years, and at one point he, too, almost died.

But he also made a friend for life. Every day, his new friend, Father Trevor Huddleston, came to talk to him. The two of them chatting was a funny sight: the small, skinny Desmond and the tall priest, who himself later became an archbishop. Trevor Huddleston brought Desmond books to read and inspired him with a lifelong devotion to Christianity.

The apartheid election

In 1948, disaster struck for all black South Africans. A general election was held in the country, and Whites, who were the only people allowed to vote, chose the openly racist National Party to lead the country. It had campaigned with a new slogan, "apartheid" (literally "apart-hood"), and promised to introduce extreme anti-Black policies.

It was a fateful decision. At a time when the rest of the world was pulling back from the tragedies of World War II and the Holocaust, the white people of South Africa were moving in the opposite direction.

Though racism, segregation, and oppression of Blacks by Whites in South Africa had been going on for centuries, things quickly became much worse under the new government. It immediately set to work passing a flurry of evil new laws. Racial prejudice and persecution of Blacks became a central part of the law of the land.

First came the Prohibition of Mixed Marriages Act and the Immorality Act, which together made sex and marriage between Whites and "Non-whites" illegal. Then there was the Population Registration Act, under which every person in the country was arbitrarily classified by skin color: White, "Coloured" (the term created for people regarded as neither White nor Black), Asian, or "Native" (the word Whites used at the time for Blacks).

Classification under the Population Registration Act of 1950 was at first into four "racial" groups but later laws made classification even more complicated. "Coloureds" were further divided into subcategories — Cape Coloured, Cape Malay, Griqua, Asian, Chinese, Other Asiatic, Other Coloured. Africans were subdivided into eight groups according to language. Whites remained as only one category despite any differences in their cultural and ethnic origins — for example, English, Afrikaners, Portuguese, Greeks, Japanese, Hungarians, Jews, and Poles.

The word "race" originally meant "a group that shared a common ancestor." But nineteenth-century biologists came up with a theory that human beings could be split into different groups or "races." The study of genetics, or heredity, has shown that the

"I wrote to the [prime minister] about what I could only call a diabolical policy — this policy of Black uprooting . . . basically he was saying the removals are legal. Here in South Africa we tend to think that legal and morally right mean the same thing."

Desmond Tutu,
in Hope and Suffering

In the 1950s, children demonstrated against the hated Group Areas Act. The law forces Blacks, Whites, and so-called "Coloureds" to live in separate parts of the country. The banner says "We want to live with all races."

17

ADMITTED
RIGHT OF ADMISSION RESERVED

NON EUROPEANS NOT
NO DOGS ALLOWED
DO NOT DAMAGE TREES/PLANTS

MEREDALE
PLEASURE RESO(
and (PTY L
CARAVAN PARI

Apartheid is blatantly racist. This "Whites only" vacation resort at Meredale is just thirty miles (forty-eight km) from Sharpeville. As apartheid became law in the years after 1948, signs banning Blacks from "Whites only" beaches, park benches, buses, and other public places appeared throughout the country. Now many signs have been removed, but the attitude they represent remains.

differences between people within a given population group are enormous compared with the differences between population groups themselves. Thus, the idea of different "races" has no real meaning for humans. "Race" is literally skin-deep! Or if you want to use the word in its original meaning, we all belong to only one race — the human race.

In South Africa's case, you can see the nonsense that arises when you try to sort people of many ethnic backgrounds into different "races." During the first ten years of the Act the Population Board tried thousands of cases. Behind these statistics lie broken families and untold heartache.

The Group Areas Act, which said each "race" had to live in a different place, and the Bantu Authorities Act were passed, setting up "dumping grounds" for black groups that Whites didn't want to have living near them. Schools, the use of public transportation, public toilets, even park benches were divided by race.

It was the beginning of a nightmare.

By 1950, Desmond had graduated from high school with distinction. The Blacks lived under dreadful conditions, and one of them included poor or nonexistent educational opportunities. Tutu was one of the few Blacks who was able to enter a university. His first goal, having seen the physical suffering around him, was to become a doctor. But there was no money for him to study medicine, so he followed in his father's footsteps and became a teacher.

During this period, he met the woman he was to marry, Leah Nomalizo Shenxane, who was also a teacher. She had been one of his father's brightest pupils. At first, the studious Desmond barely noticed her. But as he grew to know her, he fell in love and asked her to marry him. In 1955 Desmond and Leah married, and soon they had their first of four children. They named him Trevor, after Tutu's friend, Father Trevor Huddleston.

By this time, Desmond had earned a B.A. (Bachelor of Arts) degree. He had also become an exceptional and inspiring teacher at the Munsieville High School in Krugersdorp. Up to sixty students per class would listen spellbound to his lessons.

It looked as though Tutu had found his true vocation. But he would not enjoy his new profession long.

"[Dr. Verwoerd] said that since we could feed only some [black children] and not all, we must not feed even those we could. . . . Because you can't cure all TB patients don't cure those you can — would that be acceptable?"

Desmond Tutu,
in Hope and Suffering

Desmond and Leah Tutu on their wedding day, July 2, 1955. Leah was a powerful person in her own right. She would bring a sense of peace and happiness to Desmond in the years ahead.

19

In 1955, the South African government finally turned its attention to black schools and introduced the Bantu Education Act.

The Bantu Education Act was one of the most unjust of all the new laws. It was the brainchild of one of the most sinister apartheid leaders to appear in South Africa's history, Dr. Hendrik Verwoerd. The purpose of this "education" law was actually to stop anyone from teaching black children anything they might need to learn. Blacks, Verwoerd was determined, were to have a deliberately inferior education.

He wanted no more smart, well-educated black people in South Africa. As far as he was concerned, the only job a black person was fit for was as a servant to Whites. "What is the use of teaching the Bantu child mathematics when it cannot use it in practice?" Verwoerd had asked. He added, "If the Native in South Africa today is being taught to expect that he will live his adult life under a policy of equal rights, he is making a big mistake."

Black South Africa recoiled at this overtly expressed racism. Desmond and others committed to black education were horrified by these statements. He could not tolerate being a teacher if the Bantu Education Act were to be enforced.

So he turned to his faith to solve his problem. His family had always been religious and he was already a passionately committed Christian. Greatly influenced by people like Trevor Huddleston, he decided to join a theological college and become a priest.

He was one day to say, about his role as a clergyman and as a world religious leader: "I was grabbed by God by the scruff of the neck in order to spread His word, whether it is convenient or not."

Peaceful protest

From the very first day the apartheid laws were enacted, courageous peoples from all cultural groups had protested against this cruel and inhuman system.

The first joint campaign of defiance was planned by the African National Congress (ANC) and the South African Indian Council (SAIC). It was led by brilliant and brave leaders like Albert John Luthuli, Oliver Tambo, and Nelson Mandela.

Until the 1970s, Blacks often had to build their own schools. On the wall behind this student, who lives in the Eastern Transvaal, you can see the patterns children's fingers have made in the mud as they worked. Many students are too poor to buy schoolbooks.

Ever since the ANC was formed in 1912, protest against injustice had been peaceful. The new campaign was no different, though it was more widespread and passionate than anything the country had ever seen before. The protests followed the principles of "nonviolence" developed and first used in South Africa by Mahatma Gandhi forty years before. Later Gandhi put it into successful practice against British rule in India. This method of peaceful protest became a model for Dr. Martin Luther King, Jr. in the United States. It would later be adopted by Desmond Tutu.

"Freedom and liberty lose out by default because good people are not vigilant."
Desmond Tutu,
in Hope and Suffering

The aim of the Defiance Campaign was to make everyone, especially those in authority, realize how inhuman, unfair, and stupid the apartheid laws were. To shame the government into changing the law, protesters tried filling the prisons to overflowing. They hoped to demonstrate that the law literally imprisoned an entire people.

Thousands of volunteers joined together to break laws like the ones that made it illegal for Blacks to walk in white cities at night. But they might be called law-abiding protesters. They were always careful to tell the police in advance which laws they were going to break. And when they had broken them, they demanded to be arrested and put in prison! They also made sure that journalists were always there to see and report what happened.

The various congress movements, including the ANC as well as "coloured" and white opponents of apartheid, now united to form the National Action Council of the Congress of the People. In 1955 this group published a "Freedom Charter" calling for an end to hunger, discrimination, and injustice. The charter demanded votes for all men and women and an equal share of the country's wealth.

Then, in 1956, the government arrested 156 Congress members of all backgrounds and colors. These leaders were then put on trial for treason. This famous trial lasted four seemingly endless years. After all that time, the charges were dropped against Congress members or they were found not guilty.

The trial brought apartheid to the attention of the world. But it was soon to be overshadowed by the first of many bloody tragedies.

Vernon Barrange, a lawyer defending members of Congress at the Treason Trial, is carried shoulder high after their victory in 1961. All the defendants were found "not guilty." This four-year trial brought the problems in South Africa to the attention of the world. The South African government had been publicly humiliated.

The Sharpeville Massacre shocked the world. On March 21, 1960, sixty-nine men and women were shot dead by police during a peaceful demonstration against the hated Pass Laws. In South Africa, the police routinely use violence to discourage nonviolent protest.

"Don't delay our freedom, which is your freedom as well, for freedom is indivisible."

Desmond Tutu,
in Hope and Suffering

Massacre at Sharpeville

It was March 21, 1960. Five thousand peaceful demonstrators gathered outside a police station in the South African township of Sharpeville. They were there to protest the Pass Laws. In the crowd there were many women and children.

Without warning, the police opened fire. Screams of terror rang through the air. The crowd turned and fled in panic, but the police kept on shooting. When all had grown quiet, sixty-nine men and women lay dead in the dusty street, and 180 were wounded. It was a horrible incident in South Africa's history. Worse yet, it would not be the only time policemen would shoot unarmed black demonstrators without warning.

The Sharpeville Massacre shocked the world. It was followed by weeks of protests and strikes by Blacks. But neither the protests nor public attention loosened the grip of apartheid. The government, as it has usually done ever since, reacted to serious opposition with more repression. It outlawed the ANC and the other main black resistance movement, the Pan-Africanist Congress (PAC). Many opponents of apartheid were put in prison without trial. While held in prison, they were often tortured. The police paid a huge network of Blacks to spy on other Blacks. They wanted to know the movements of anyone suspected of opposing the government's policies.

Blacks and a significant number of Whites who opposed apartheid were frustrated by the failure of their campaign. They had tried passive, nonviolent resistance, and they were shocked by the killings at Sharpeville. For almost fifty years, the ANC had used only peaceful means to make its protests. But now certain members of the group were growing impatient. Under the leadership of Nelson Mandela, the ANC set up a military wing that was called *Umkhonto we Sizwe,* or "Spear of the Nation."

Members of the Umkhonto were not to attack people but were only to sabotage places like electricity substations. Some members carried out bomb attacks, which were largely ineffective. *Poqo*, which means "standing alone," was the name of the military wing of the PAC. It was a more violent group.

By the end of 1964, both Umkhonto and Poqo had been destroyed. The police captured all the leaders of Umkhonto at a house in Rivonia, a suburb of Johannesburg, and put them on trial. Mandela, a man who had never killed anyone, was jailed for life. Today he is still in prison and speaks to the world through his wife, Winnie Mandela, who has also become a leader against apartheid.

Some ANC leaders, like Oliver Tambo, fled South Africa to keep the organization alive. But most of the other leaders were jailed along with Mandela.

Nelson Mandela, leader of the African National Congress (ANC). Since 1962, he has been serving a life sentence in prison. To many Blacks, he is still South Africa's rightful leader. Many people of all colors around the world have campaigned for his release.

Tutu goes to London

Meanwhile, Tutu was committed to his work in the Church. He showed no signs of the outspoken political views that would one day make him famous. For three years he had studied theology and had been ordained as a priest. He had been the star pupil at the seminary. So in 1962, at thirty-one, Desmond left South Africa to go to London to study theology at King's College and to work as an assistant curate.

There, far away from the growing misery in his own country, he fell in love with a new world. It took him and Leah a while to get used to the northern weather but compared to South Africa, London seemed to them like paradise.

Back home, every policeman on the street was a potential enemy who might ask to see their passbooks or who might make life unpleasant in other ways. By comparison, the British police seemed amazingly polite. Desmond and Leah could hardly believe it. Sometimes they walked around central London late at night just for the pleasure of *not* being arrested! In their new freedom, they found pleasure in stopping policemen to ask for directions, even when they knew where they were going.

One day Desmond was waiting in line at a bank when a white man pushed in front of him. The cashier politely told the bully that he would have to wait his turn because Desmond was first. Desmond was astonished! This basic kind of respect would never have happened in South Africa.

He was also surprised at the freedom British people had to express their opinions. To his pleasure, he discovered Speakers' Corner in London's Hyde Park. Anyone who had anything to say could come to this corner and express any opinion. And the policemen were on duty to *protect* the speakers, even though some of them were saying the most outrageous things. At home, in South Africa, these people would have been quickly arrested.

At King's College he was popular. He quickly became a star student, getting first a bachelor's degree in 1965, and then, just a year later, a master's degree in theology. He added Hebrew to the seven languages he already knew — Xhosa, Tswana, Venda, Zulu, English, Afrikaans, and Greek.

He was also well loved at the churches where he worked. His clowning, his powerful preaching, his kindness, and his extroverted style relaxed the usually formal British people. They were amused when he would tear around the parish on his motorcycle. When it came time for Desmond and Leah to leave England there were many tears at the huge farewell party given in their honor.

24

Tutu learned a great deal during his four years in England about religion and politics — and kindness, which he gave and received in huge quantities. This also confirmed what he already knew — that black and white people could easily live together without conflict or bitterness if they chose to. But it was time for him to go home.

Police state

While Desmond was away, apartheid had mercilessly tightened its grip. Dr. Hendrik Verwoerd, apartheid's sinister leader, had become Prime Minister in 1958.

At that time apartheid policies were incomplete. Some areas of life were as yet unaffected by apartheid laws. Blacks and Whites still even lived together in a few areas of the country and sometimes played professional sports together.

Verwoerd was determined to change that. He was a fanatical racist. Like many Afrikaners, he believed that Whites would be contaminated or corrupted by coming too closely into contact with Blacks. He was obsessed with people's color and imagined the "white race" was in danger and needed to be protected if it was to survive. In fact, the truth was the other way around. The people who needed protection were Blacks. They urgently needed to be protected from apartheid and Dr. Verwoerd!

In 1960, the British prime minister, Harold Macmillan, made a famous speech in South Africa criticizing apartheid and saying that a "wind of change" was blowing through Africa. But there wasn't much practical help offered from the outside. As before, the South African people had to face the apartheid storm mainly on their own.

After Sharpeville, Verwoerd unleashed a police assault on any remaining civil liberties in the country. New, even harsher apartheid laws meant strict segregation in every area of life. Black people were banned from "white" buses, beaches, toilets, and sports fields. Blacks had to have special permission to be out of their immediate area. If they didn't they would be arrested and put into prison.

But Verwoerd's new laws about the places where black people could live had the most profound effects.

[Desmond] told us how the police can knock at the door and take away the husband or the wife, and if a neighbor doesn't happen to see, that person has just gone . . . they just disappear."
John Ewington, a friend of Desmond Tutu's, from Shirley du Boulay's book Tutu: Voice of the Voiceless

"How do we compute the cost [of apartheid] in the legacy of bitterness, anger, frustration and indeed hatred which we are leaving behind for our children?"
Desmond Tutu, in Hope and Suffering

He declared that because people of different "races" were "different" they should "develop separately." He therefore offered Blacks "independence" in their own lands, or "Bantustans." Most Blacks had never even seen their so-called "homelands." The new law was just an excuse to expel them from white areas and banish them to the poorest, most infertile areas of the country. The Bantustans were just huge slums.

Whites seized most of the country and all the best land for themselves, leaving only 13 percent specifically for the other groups who made up 80 percent of the population. Then South Africa's white government made things even worse. The government used the law to give itself power to kick Blacks out of their homes to make way for Whites. Blacks were now not citizens of South Africa. They were treated like migrant laborers.

Under the Group Areas Act entire black populations were "removed" from places where they had lived for generations. Between 1960 and 1983, more than three million people were dragged off or forced to leave their homes. If the people refused to move, the government simply sent police with trucks and bulldozers. They smashed down their homes and physically carried the people away, dumping them in barren, faraway places as if they were sacks of potatoes.

Sophiatown

One of the places where this had happened in the early days of apartheid was Sophiatown, a black community in Johannesburg. Nearly sixty thousand people lived there, many of them in houses they owned or had built themselves. Desmond Tutu knew Sophiatown well. He had lived there when he was at school. His friend, Father Trevor Huddleston, was the priest there and together with local people, he tried to save Sophiatown from being wiped out.

But they didn't stand a chance. One day, two thousand policemen arrived with eighty trucks. When all the Blacks had been taken away, their homes were destroyed. Sophiatown was razed to the ground. In its place, the government built a new white suburb with a name which showed its contempt for its previous owners, "Triumph."

"You are told by those who are powerful . . . that you must move from your property because they want it. . . . Your community is being destroyed. You are being asked to abandon your South African citizenship. . . . It is almost as if you are being stoned to death as a community . . . "

Desmond Tutu, to a group of black villagers

26

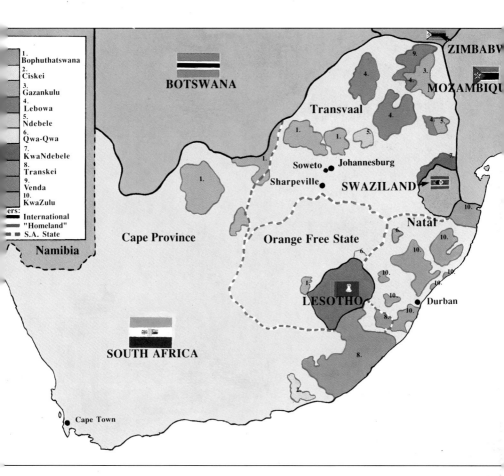

ZIMBABW

BOTSWANA

MOZAMBIQU

Transvaal

Soweto Johannesburg

Sharpeville SWAZILAND

Natal

Cape Province

Orange Free State

Namibia

LESOTHO

Durban

SOUTH AFRICA

Cape Town

Broken families

Since the 1960s Blacks have been forced to live in remote, barren, and dusty "homelands" or in ramshackle townships which are built outside the rich white towns and cities.

This division, this apartheid, has caused untold misery to millions of people. It has caused poverty and made it almost impossible for Blacks to live a decent life or to succeed in any way.

Perhaps the most tragic result of apartheid was the breakdown of family life. Thousands and thousands of people were lost in the removals. With no telephones, no money, no home ownership, it was almost impossible to find people once they'd been moved.

A person from one area who fell in love with a person from a different area was not legally allowed

The "homelands" are in fact a jigsaw of twenty-eight highly fragmented parcels of land that were left for the Africans after the Whites had expanded to occupy the best areas. The population densities in these lands are among the highest in Africa. There is little work available in these overcrowded and barren dumping grounds. The average income is also lower than in any independent African state.

27

to visit. If they were of different "races," married couples found themselves in different "homelands"!

Desperately poor black fathers, with no land or job in the Bantustans, had to go to the cities to work. Mothers could find jobs only as live-in "nannies" or "girls," domestic servants, to white families. People who did not have jobs were kept out of the cities. So the disabled, the elderly, and the children were left behind in the Bantustans. The meager salaries of the parents were sent "home."

Through these turbulent and sad years, Desmond Tutu worked his way up through the Church. He was an outstandingly brilliant scholar. When he returned from Britain, he had three degrees. His first job was as a lecturer in Greek and theology at the Federal Theological Seminary at Alice, in the Cape Province.

Tutu continued his deeply religious life, which included long hours of meditation as well as days of fasting and silence. His worship and his Christianity were deep personal commitments. But there were no signs yet that he would one day become the most famous political figure in South Africa.

Above: A mother struggles to do her household chores under miserable conditions in the Zwelitemba Township. When families are forcibly removed, they are often left to survive on barren, distant land that Whites do not want.

Opposite: This family from Sophiatown was among the victims of the forced removals to the "homelands," barren lands hundreds of miles from their real homes. Their home was then destroyed by government officials. Three and a half million Blacks have been treated this way in South Africa since the 1960s.

29

South African Blacks, Tutu included, are not allowed to eat in "white" areas. They are served through hatches, like this one, at the side or back of the building.

"To be impartial . . .
is indeed to have taken
sides already . . . with
the status quo."
              Desmond Tutu,
           in Hope and Suffering

It was not that Tutu was politically naive. He saw what was happening around him and was affected by it. The blazing injustice of the South African laws struck him every day. He realized that no matter how many degrees he earned, no matter how senior he became, no matter how honest he was or how good, he still would not be able to sit at a table to eat in a "white" café, no matter how filthy the café. He had to go around to the side and be served from an area set aside for "non-whites." He would never be able to send his children to a white school, which was often the school with the best equipment and faculty, nor could he own a home in a white area. He could not vote. Yet Tutu continued to put religion first, and though the demands on his time, emotions, and energy grew as the years passed, this never changed.

Turning point

A dreadful incident in 1968 was one of the major turning points in Desmond's life.

While he was lecturing at Alice, he also worked as the chaplain at Fort Hare University, one of only three universities for black students in South Africa at the time. It was the year student revolution broke out in the United States and Europe, and the students at Fort Hare staged their own less aggressive strikes and protests, asking for very moderate improvements in the way the university was being run.

At one point, five hundred of the students were holding a peaceful sit-in on the university lawns. It was a very mild protest compared with the riots and mass marches that had taken place in France, West Germany, and the United States.

During the morning the students were warned that they should abandon the protest by two that afternoon or face expulsion. They continued to sit, quietly talking and reading. At two o'clock the police arrived and reacted with terrifying brutality, tearing into the students with armored cars, dogs, and tear gas. At gunpoint, the students were made to collect their belongings and leave.

In a land where just gaining the opportunity to get a university education meant long years of sacrifice for all black students, this was a horrible punishment.

"'Does your mother receive a pension or grant or something?'
'No,' she replied.
'Then what do you do for food?'
'We borrow food,' she answered.
'Have you ever returned any of the food you have borrowed?'
'No.'
'What do you do when you can't borrow food?'
'We drink water to fill our stomachs.'"
Desmond Tutu, in conversation with a young black girl of the Zweleding resettlement camp, quoted in Shirley du Boulay's book
Tutu: Voice of the Voiceless

The Tutu family in London, where Desmond studied for his theology degree. Desmond and Leah with their four children — left to right: Trevor, Theresa, Naomi, and Mpho.

The incident made it practically impossible for the victims to go to a university ever again. It certainly ruined many lives.

Desmond was deeply shocked. Until that point, he had been quite unpolitical in his views, but now he threw himself into the thick of the trouble by standing up for the protesting students.

Tutu was shaken to the core by the violent attack on peaceful protesters. Nearly twenty years later, he remembered: "I never felt so desolate. . . . I was angry with God. I couldn't understand how He could let all that happen to those students."

Dean of Johannesburg

After two years as a lecturer in Alice, Tutu moved to the small country of Lesotho, where he taught at the University of Botswana, Lesotho, and Swaziland. By the early 1970s, he was already well known within the Anglican Church in southern Africa. He was a respected scholar and determined to rise rapidly within the church hierarchy.

Between 1972-75, Tutu again worked in London, this time as the associate director of the Theological Education Fund. During these years he visited many countries to allocate funds. He saw many of the world's troubled areas and gained wide experience that would prove to be invaluable to him in the turbulent years ahead.

His reputation was growing with every passing year, and his kindness, wisdom, and courage became widely known. Increasingly, he began to speak out against the injustice that he saw all around him.

In 1975, Tutu was catapulted to prominence when he was elected the Dean of Johannesburg. No Black had ever been appointed to such a senior position in the Anglican Church before. From this time on, any speech he uttered would be heard — and quoted. It was a very public position.

Black people were excited, delighted, and proud of him. They were even more pleased with one of Desmond's first decisions. He showed his support for fellow Blacks by refusing to move into the plush home in a white suburb where previous deans had lived. Instead, he and his family would live twelve miles (nineteen km) away from his cathedral — in Soweto, the sprawling, slum-ridden black township where most of the Blacks who worked in Johannesburg lived.

But Desmond, so full of life and energy, never let himself be depressed by these grim surroundings. Some white members of his new church, St. Mary's Cathedral, were surprised by the warm way he led worship. They certainly weren't used to being asked to hug and kiss each other!

Letter to the Prime Minister

It was then that Tutu took his first controversial political step that would rocket him to fame in South Africa. Tutu, aware of the tensions building up in the townships, especially among young people, wrote a very polite and respectful open letter "as one Christian to another" to the new Prime Minister, John Vorster. In it he appealed for justice and an end to racial oppression in South Africa. "I write to you, Sir, because, like you, I am deeply committed to real reconciliation with justice for all, and to peaceful change to a more just and open South African society in which the wonderful wealth and riches of our country will be shared more equitably."

He prophesied that without justice and freedom for Blacks, all South Africans, both Black and White, faced a terrible and bloody future.

"I have a growing nightmarish fear that unless something drastic is done very soon then bloodshed and violence are going to happen in South Africa almost inevitably."

Black people, he said, could "take only so much and no more. . . . A people made desperate by despair, injustice and oppression will use desperate means. I am frightened, dreadfully frightened, that we may soon reach a point of no return, when events will generate a momentum of their own, when nothing will stop their reaching a bloody dénouement which is 'too ghastly to contemplate.'"

He pleaded with Vorster to end the Pass Laws and let black people live in "white" cities. He urged Vorster to talk to black leaders and to try to understand their views.

Vorster virtually ignored the letter. He refused to

"Blacks don't want crumbs of concessions from the master's table. They want to be there determining the menu together."
Desmond Tutu,
in Hope and Suffering

Apartheid deprives Blacks of rights that other people take for granted, such as the right to live and work where they want. This couple was fired for arguing with another worker. Having been fired, they and their family immediately became homeless and illegal. If they can't find work, they must go to a "homeland," where the land is poor, and they will probably become impoverished.

Soweto, June 16, 1976: Children sing and dance in peaceful protest of a new law that says their lessons must be taught in Afrikaans rather than their native language.

answer Tutu's arguments and wrote back accusing him of trying to "make propaganda."

But the terrible events that Tutu predicted were to come true even sooner than anyone in South Africa and the rest of the world had thought possible.

The children of Soweto

For several years, a new political movement had been growing among young Blacks. It was called "Black Consciousness." It encouraged Blacks to be proud of their history and culture and to consider themselves equal to Whites. These young people were politically alert and aware of the humiliations suffered by their parents' generation. They were determined not to suffer so patiently.

Then in 1976, just a month and a half after Tutu's prophetic letter, the spark was lit. The government had made an amazingly tactless move. They ordered that lessons in black schools should not be taught in English but instead should be taught in Afrikaans, the

"English newspapers . . . would describe an accident in these words: 'Three persons and a Native were injured.'"

Desmond Tutu,
in Hope and Suffering

34

The same demonstration, less than an hour later. The police have opened fire and twelve-year-old Hector Peterson is dead. He is the first of nearly six hundred children to be killed in what became a mass uprising that shook South Africa for months.

long-hated language of the white oppressors.

At first the student protests were quiet and peaceful. As usual, they were ignored by the government. Then, on the fateful day of June 16, 1976, black schoolchildren gathered in the dusty streets of Soweto and marched from school to school, their numbers growing rapidly. Finally, a singing, laughing, excited crowd of ten to fifteen thousand children waving placards converged on the Orlando sports stadium.

The reaction of the police was the most terrible since the massacre at Sharpeville. They opened fire on the children. A twelve-year-old boy named Hector Peterson was the first of many to be killed. Over the next few weeks, hundreds of other youngsters all over the country died as more young Blacks rioted in

"My vision is of a South Africa that is totally non-racial. It will be a society that is more just. . . . Freedom is indivisible. Whites can't enjoy their separate freedoms. They spend too much time and resources defending those freedoms instead of enjoying them."

Desmond Tutu,
in Hope and Suffering

After 1976, young Blacks began to lead the struggle against apartheid. They were determined not to be servile like their parents. This young woman is proud to be black.

sympathy for the Soweto children and in defiance of the requirement that they be taught in Afrikaans.

The demonstrations in Soweto quickly escalated into a national black uprising against apartheid led by the schoolchildren. There had never been anything like it during all the years of protest.

After several months and many hundreds of deaths and thousands of injuries, the uprising eventually came to an end. It failed to bring an end to apartheid, but it had shaken the system to its foundations. People all over the world were outraged by the savagery of the police and soldiers. Repeated scenes of police opening fire with automatic rifles on small groups of unarmed, singing students had an electrifying effect on the world. Attention was once again focused on South Africa, to the dismay of its white leaders.

Desmond Tutu was unable to be with his people through this tragic period. In 1976, after less than two

Opposite: Blacks rioted against apartheid for months after the killings at Soweto. White policemen patrolled the turbulent townships in armored cars, trying to put down the uprising (top), while young Blacks continued to vent their anger on the streets (bottom).

37

Inches away, but worlds apart. White schoolboys leaving a cadet camp in Vereeniging pass a group of young Blacks their own age. Because of the apartheid laws, these white boys are not allowed to see how Blacks live in their own land. Unfortunately, the only way black boys will see inside white homes is if they are servants.

years as Dean of Johannesburg, he was consecrated Bishop of Lesotho, the small, independent country surrounded by South Africa. He had, in fact, agreed to the appointment before he wrote to Vorster that May.

It was frustrating and heartbreaking to be away from his people during these troubled days, but Desmond Tutu committed himself fully to his work as bishop. It was another vital part of his training for his future role in the world.

When Steven Biko, the founder and leader of the Black Consciousness Movement, was murdered by the South African police, Tutu was called back to speak at his funeral. It was an event full of anguish. Biko had been a wise and gifted man. Although he was only thirty years old when he died, it seemed he had been ready to become the greatest South African black leader since Nelson Mandela.

Biko's death from beatings and torture at the hands of police had been a shattering blow that shocked all freedom-loving South Africans and the rest of the world. Desmond's words expressed their feelings: "We are numb with grief, and groan with anguish 'Oh

God, where are you? Oh God, do you really care —
how can you let this happen to us?'" Desmond had not
met Steven Biko, but he shared the dream of making
Africans proud, equal, and able to achieve a real peace
and equality with Whites.

Prayer for white people too

Desmond also passionately believed that apartheid
damaged Whites as well as Blacks because it made
them lose their humanity. South Africa's Minister of
Justice, Jimmy Kruger, had shown just how shock-
ingly true this was when he said that Biko's death
"leaves me cold." Of all human beings, Kruger was
"the most to be pitied," said Desmond. "What has
happened to him as a human being when the death of
a fellow human being can leave him cold?"

So he asked the mourners at Biko's funeral to pray
for the white people of South Africa, for the rulers and
the police, especially the security police who had murdered Steven Biko so that they, too, "may realize they
are human beings."

Tutu's words were not popular with everyone at the
funeral because people were enraged over what had
happened to Steven Biko. Despite their anger, Tutu
made them look at the way that white people in South
Africa are also victims of apartheid.

It may seem hard to believe, but many Whites in
South Africa have no clear idea about what life is like
for Blacks. For instance, white children who have
black nannies to love and look after them, and who
have dozens of expensive toys to play with, simply
cannot imagine what life is like for black children in
the same country. They don't see how black people
live because white people are not allowed to go into
the townships or so-called "homelands." In the same
way that ancient Romans thought that owning slaves
was perfectly normal, white South Africans are also
brought up to think that separating people because of
their "race" is a sensible, good thing.

What makes things worse is that South African
radio and television stations are so heavily censored
by the government that they give a very peculiar
impression of the world. People in other countries
know more about the injustice in South Africa than

*"The first step . . . is to
make the black man come
to himself; to pump back
life into his empty shell;
to infuse him with pride
and dignity, to remind
him of his complicity in
the crime of allowing
himself to be misused and
therefore letting evil reign
supreme in the country of
his birth."*

Steven Biko,
I Write What I Like

39

"Apartheid comprehensively contradicts the Bible and Christian teaching. That is why it is totally evil and totally immoral." Bishop Desmond Tutu is a passionate preacher, respected for his knowledge of theology.

South Africans themselves. As in many closed political systems, much money is spent on propaganda. Though every protest or act of hooliganism in Europe is shown on South African television, the black South African riots do not appear. Problems in other African countries are shown, but similar problems in South Africa are just not shown.

One of the most tragic effects of all these years of propaganda was that it had worked on *all* people. Black people also thought of themselves as inferior; they saw few successful black leaders to look up to. People such as Steven Biko and Desmond Tutu helped to counter this. There was now a growing confidence and pride among Blacks. Asians and "Coloureds" now wanted to be called "Black." Blacks saw that it was necessary to stop the government strategy of "divide and rule" if they were to unite South Africa.

One example of this deliberately slanted news reporting is the unfair and distorted way Desmond Tutu is shown on television in his own country. His wit, love, and lack of bitterness shine through when he preaches or gives interviews. But South African television usually edits his appearances to give viewers the idea that he must be a slightly crazy, bitter revolutionary. If he gives an hour-long talk on preventing a bloodbath, he will be shown waving his arms vigorously (as he regularly does!) while the commentator talks. Then Tutu's voice will sound for just one phrase: "there is going to be a bloodbath."

He is regularly misquoted by newspapers.

Nothing could be more unfair. All his life, Tutu has believed in and preached for love, peace, and reconciliation. He believes that apartheid is a completely evil system. He says that because God created all people equal, laws and acts that allow one group to discriminate against others are blasphemous crimes against God. This, above all, is why he cannot separate religion from politics.

He has often shown anger over injustice, but he has never shown hatred for white people. Like most black people, he simply yearns for the day when apartheid is gone and all South Africans can live together happily as equals at peace without resentment or violence on either side. The tragedy is that most South Africans never hear what he is actually trying to say to them.

> *"If apartheid is dead, then urgent funeral arrangements need to be made. The body is still around and it is making a terrible smell."*
> Percy Qoboza, Editor
> The Post *(Johannesburg)*

Into the hot seat

In 1978, after just two years as Bishop of Lesotho, Tutu was given a very important and highly controversial job. Again, he felt compelled to take it. He returned from Lesotho to South Africa. This time he was returning for good.

The new job was to last six years and would be his most demanding and politically sensitive yet. He was appointed the first black general secretary of the South African Council of Churches (SACC). He remained a bishop, but without a diocese, though he was still the man with the highest position in the South African Anglican church. It was a time when South Africans again felt unrest, and the churches were becoming increasingly outspoken in their attacks on apartheid.

After the uprising in Soweto and the death of Steven Biko, the South African government knew it had to make some changes in the apartheid system. Over the

next few years the black middle class continued to grow rapidly. Businesses needed all the talented people they could get. Despite the government's laws, people were making attempts to ignore apartheid. It looked as though the country might grow out of the oppressive system.

Some of the most obvious symbols of apartheid were indeed abolished. For instance, the laws that forbade Blacks to go to "Whites-only" public parks and toilets were scrapped. Black and white athletes played sports together in a way that would have been punishable a few years earlier. Blacks were now allowed to set foot inside "international hotels" in the cities. Even government representatives seemed to be showing sensitivity to the living conditions for South Africa's Blacks. The new prime minister, P. W. Botha, warned Whites that apartheid without any reforms, even minor ones, could lead to disaster. "Adapt or die," he told his fellow white South Africans. His words made headlines worldwide.

But they proved, in fact, to be hollow words. The government had no real intention of getting rid of the fundamental basis of apartheid. Great reforms were promised. Afrikaner politicians were aware of South Africa's terrible reputation in the world, so they tried to persuade the world that apartheid was becoming a thing of the past. But the cruel Pass Laws and Group Areas Act remained intact. Thousands of black people were still being evicted from their homes. Blacks were still denied basic political rights.

In any case, the improvements that took place would hardly have been enough to satisfy an angry new generation of young Blacks. After the uprising in Soweto, young Blacks were feeling brave and determined. They were impatient for change. They would never again accept apartheid as their parents had accepted it in the past. Of course, such determination made many Whites uneasy. Members of the government realized they would only be able to keep control over Blacks by resorting to more brutal and oppressive methods than they had used in the past. Blacks began to realize even more clearly that they would have to fight back if their freedom movement was to survive white attempts to withhold their basic rights.

"There's a natural antagonism among the majority of white South Africans at having to pay obeisance to a black man, be he a Bishop or not. And it is very hard for many of them ... to get used to the idea of having a black man in command of a very important section of their lives. That, of course, is pure racist, but you can't ignore it in this country."
Helen Suzman,
quoted by
Shirley du Boulay in
Tutu: Voice of the Voiceless

Opposite: A vision of the future? This multiracial class is becoming common in South Africa. It offers a glimpse of how the country might be after apartheid is abolished. It also confirms Desmond Tutu's vision of racial peace and harmony.

Tutu's rising voice

Against this upheaval, Desmond Tutu was becoming a world figure and one of the best known of all the voices of South African protest.

He had always been first and foremost a religious person rather than a politician, but in his new job he showed he could also be a fearless and tireless campaigner. In almost every speech, article, sermon, and interview in South Africa and abroad, he denounced apartheid and called for justice. He demanded an end to tyranny. He spoke of God as an activist: "God . . . takes sides. He is not a neutral God. He took the side of the slaves, the oppressed, the victims."

He never preached violence. Instead, his message, repeated over and over again with his remarkable gift for words and his unequaled passion as an orator, was one of reason, peace, and reconciliation.

"An insect in dark glasses"

Nevertheless, many white people wished he would "keep politics out of religion." They didn't like having a black bishop telling them that they were partly responsible for South Africa's problems. Tutu became the target of increasingly cruel and unfair attacks from government leaders and from South African media that tried to portray him as a violent and dangerous revolutionary. Many of these attacks were spiteful as well as ridiculous. One newspaper cruelly referred to him as "an insect in dark glasses."

There was a more sinister side to this hatred as well. Tutu began to receive anonymous death threats and abusive phone calls. Whenever this happened, Desmond startled the caller by carefully listening until the threat was over, then saying a prayer for the caller before hanging up.

Because of his outspoken opposition to apartheid, many white people seemed to think Tutu was the devil incarnate. Tutu later joked, "I really do have horns underneath my funny bishop's hat." But behind all the laughter and clowning, Desmond Tutu was an extremely sensitive man. He told friends that he loved to love and to be loved. The jibes, insults, and threats always hurt him deeply.

Desmond Tutu addresses a crowd at the funeral of fourteen victims of violence in the black township of Kwathema in 1985. In the late 1970s and early 1980s, he became one of the most eloquent voices against apartheid. He always speaks against violence and for harmony between Blacks and Whites.

Four faces of Bishop Tutu.

Top left: At prayer during
a visit to the United States
in 1984.

Bottom left: Giving an
interview to journalists.

Above: At home
in Johannesburg in 1985.

Above: Christmas, 1987 — Archbishop Tutu enjoys his own Christmas party. He has turned his home in Cape Town into a community center, where black and white children play together. Photographer Omar Badsha, who took this picture, was imprisoned without trial in 1988.

Whatever white South Africans thought of him, people in the rest of the world had started to listen to Desmond Tutu. The fact that he was a natural TV performer certainly helped! His warmth, honesty, intelligence, and sense of fun meant that almost everyone who met him liked and respected him immediately. He had become famous. Wherever he went, reporters wanted to talk with him.

Sanctions call

But his role as leader of the South African Council of Churches, the SACC, increasingly led Tutu into clashes with the government, which started to harass him.

In early 1980, his passport was taken away because, in a 1979 television interview in Denmark, he had asked the Danes to stop buying South African coal as a protest against apartheid. England's Archbishop of Canterbury and dozens of other bishops came to Desmond's defense. The government was eventually forced to give him back his passport.

Also during 1980, Tutu was arrested during a protest march and was treated like a criminal. The police photographed him, took his fingerprints, and fined him. On a visit to the United States in 1981, Tutu called apartheid "one of the most vicious systems since Nazism." Later, he discussed South Africa's problems with Pope John Paul II in Rome.

As soon as Desmond returned to South Africa, the government took away his passport again as punishment for his outspokenness. This time he was without his passport for over a year.

From now on, whenever he went to another country, he begged the world — particularly Britain, the United States, and West Germany — to stop trading with South Africa altogether.

Tough economic sanctions, he said, were the last way of putting peaceful pressure on the South African government to give up apartheid "before it is too late."

Many people, supporters as well as opponents of Tutu, expressed fear that sanctions might harm Blacks more than they would help them.

But Tutu held firm. And his calls for sanctions have caused more anger in South Africa than anything else he ever did. Some called him a "traitor," but he always defended himself by saying there was no other nonviolent way to protest, because most black leaders have been banned or jailed, even the nonviolent ones.

The government now tried to destroy the credibility of the SACC and set up the Eloff Commission to investigate its activities. But Desmond defended it fiercely. After a protracted legal inquiry, the SACC emerged more respected than ever.

In one way, all this unwelcome attention could be taken as a compliment. Government leaders attacked Desmond because they understood how popular, respected, and therefore dangerous to them he was quickly becoming.

Peace prize winner

A much greater compliment awaited him, however.

On October 15, 1984, Desmond Tutu was told he had won the Nobel Peace Prize, one of the world's most respected and prestigious awards. The award was meant as a gesture of support not only for Desmond

A black child huddles outside a "resettlement shack" (above) while police, carrying whips known as sjamboks, *supervise the area. Any protester, no matter how unthreatening, can be beaten, arrested, or even shot.*

47

and the SACC but for "all individuals and groups in South Africa who, with their concern for human dignity, fraternity and democracy, incite the admiration of the world."

That's certainly how it was taken inside his country. South Africa's black people and anti-apartheid campaigners went wild in celebration. At the SACC's offices, staff members hugged each other, laughed, and sang for hours. "Hey, we are winning!" said Desmond delightedly when he heard the news.

The prize was a fantastic boost for the anti-apartheid struggle and congratulations flooded in from all over the world: from the President of the United States, Ronald Reagan, from Pope John Paul II in the Vatican, from the Church of England's Terry Waite, from Poland's former Solidarity leader, Lech Walesa, who had himself won the prize a few years earlier, and from the then Prime Minister of India, Indira Gandhi.

To Desmond's great regret and sadness, the South African leaders in Pretoria didn't say a word about the award, let alone congratulate the prize winner. They seemed almost stunned into silence.

Bomb scare

Before the award ceremony came more wonderful news: Desmond Tutu had been elected Bishop of Johannesburg. Then came the presentation of the Nobel Peace Prize in Oslo, the capital of Norway. It was a joyous occasion, and more eventful than anyone would have wished. During four days of celebrations, thousands of students staged a beautiful and moving torchlight procession, and there was a grand festival of folk music in the churches.

But halfway through the prize banquet, there was a warning that someone had planted a bomb in the banquet hall. Desmond, his wife, Leah, the King of Norway, and all the guests had to leave their seats while police searched the building. Outside, refusing to let the interruption get in the way of a great occasion, they sang "We Shall Overcome" (led, of course, by Desmond!) and after an hour's wait, the police declared the hall safe. Everyone was allowed back inside the hall. A choir from South Africa sang the beautiful black anthem "Nkosi Sikele' iAfrika" and

Tutu finally received the prize he so richly deserved.

In his acceptance speech, he called for peace and justice in South Africa and echoed the words of Old Testament prophets Isaiah (2:4) and Micah (4:3) with the words: "Let us beat our swords into plowshares."

Bishop Desmond Tutu was now unquestionably a major figure in world affairs. He could talk on equal terms with the most powerful leaders, while the media flocked to hear him as never before. Tutu's message was sent across the world. In the United States and Europe, millions of people who had never thought about apartheid before now heard about it through him. Many nations rallied to his side.

There were other advantages too. Being a Nobel laureate also gave him much-needed protection, status, and influence at home. He was going to need it all.

Black anger erupts

In 1984, Blacks' anger, which had been simmering under the surface of repression, erupted more explosively than ever before.

Perhaps surprisingly, the trigger for the new wave of unrest was a suggested reform. Prime Minister Botha had put forward a plan to give so-called "Coloureds" and Indians a vote for the first time in decades, though only for their own separate parliaments. It was not a very tempting offer. The Whites would still keep all the real power for themselves.

For Blacks the plan was worse than an insult. Although they were the vast majority of the population, they were totally ignored by the proposed reform. The government claimed that Blacks were not even citizens of South Africa! This was because, in the 1970s, the government had said that South African Blacks were citizens of the Bantustans, the so-called "independent" black "homelands," scattered throughout the poorer areas of the country.

This was an absurd idea. Most Blacks had never even visited the "homelands" they were supposed to belong to, and no other country in the world recognized the "homelands" as independent republics, because they simply weren't.

Black resentment could no longer be contained. Demonstrations erupted everywhere, and the protests

These schoolchildren were among three thousand who marched on government offices to protest after black homes in Tsakane were destroyed by government officials in 1985.

Members of the multi-racial United Democratic Front (UDF) mourn their dead. Mass funerals like this one have become a focus for political protest.

lasted for months. As before, the police and army reacted with violence.

In March 1985, twenty-five years after the Sharpeville Massacre, there was yet another massacre. Nineteen unarmed demonstrators were shot dead by police at Uitenhage, in the extreme south of the country. South Africa was engulfed in a seemingly endless wave of protests, riots, and strikes, which were all met by the police with arrests, detentions, and the use of shotguns, tear gas, or rhinoceros-hide whips called *sjamboks*. Police roamed the townships in their riot vehicles, adding to the atmosphere of terror. No one was safe, not even the young. Thousands of people,

including children, were locked up in jail without trial.

There was a terrifying new element as well. Radical young Blacks in the townships calling themselves "comrades" were now venting their fury and frustration on those older Blacks they accused of "collaborating" with apartheid.

A cruel new method of killing came to symbolize their anger. The dreaded "necklace" was a gasoline-filled car tire that was put over victims' heads and set on fire. Dozens of people were murdered in this horrible way. Black community leaders, policemen, and informers feared for their own lives. Almost every time there was a demonstration, someone was killed.

Above: More violence erupts as the police and army fail to break the spirit of black resistance. In 1988, the most brutal and repressive laws South Africa had ever seen were enacted to prevent protest. Even reporting violence could mean imprisonment without trial.

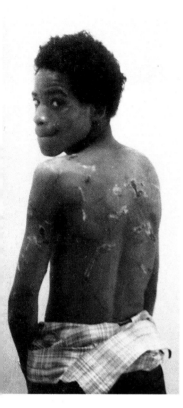

Thirty thousand people were arrested, many without charges, including thousands of children. Some were tortured. Others are still being held. The police have refused to tell families where their children are.

Desmond, who was in the thick of things making speeches, conducting gigantic funerals that became political rallies, was appalled. His dream of a peaceful end to apartheid, or as he now put it, "a *reasonably* peaceful" end to apartheid, seemed but a dim possibility. "Why," he asked, "don't we use methods of which we will be proud when our liberation is attained? This undermines the struggle."

"I will pack my bags"

One day in July 1985, Desmond came to the unhappy township of Duduza in the Transvaal for the funeral of four men who had been killed by police.

In the protests that followed, Duduza had become a sullen, scarred, and angry battleground. In one week, the police had killed ten Blacks and they had also set fire to the homes of the activists. Most of the homes of black policemen and local leaders had also been burned by angry crowds of Blacks themselves.

Now Desmond Tutu begged the mourners to turn away from violence and to try to change apartheid by peaceful means, but the crowd ignored his words. Suddenly they spotted a black man they thought was a police spy and surged forward to kill him, setting fire to his car and shouting, "Let the dog die!"

Desmond pleaded with them to no avail. Killing was wrong whatever the provocation, he said. They would not listen to him. He had to act. While two other bishops created a diversion, Desmond put his life on the line and flung himself into the seething crowd, dragging the terrified and bleeding man to safety.

A few days later, after Tutu had left, there was another funeral in Duduza. The crowd thought that a young mother named Maki Shosana also spied on her own people for the white police. A screaming mob turned on her and beat and burned her to death in full view of the television cameras. Horrifying pictures of the killing were seen across the world.

Tutu was shocked. In a packed sports stadium in KwaThema, where he was conducting yet another funeral, he spoke his mind.

"If you do that kind of thing again I will find it difficult to speak for the cause of liberation," he warned. "If the violence continues, I will pack my

bags, collect my family and leave this beautiful country that I love so passionately.... Our cause is just and noble. That is why it will prevail and bring victory to us. You cannot use methods to attain the goal of liberation that our enemy will use against us."

Such views made Tutu unpopular with impatient, radical Blacks. They were also angry that Tutu agreed to meet P. W. Botha, now President under South Africa's 1984 constitution, during the crisis. Tutu insisted that true peace could come only through dialogue, and that even the leader of such an inhuman government was a human being. Unpopular as he was with some Blacks, Tutu was even more unpopular with the white South African government.

Meanwhile President Botha had declared a "state of emergency," giving the police and army savage new powers of repression and imposing severe restrictions on the media. South Africa was more of a police state than ever before.

Bishop Tutu holds an all-night vigil to save the people and the small village of Mogopa. Though they had lived there for generations, the next day the whole town was bulldozed and the people were forcibly taken away. White farmers bought the villagers' cattle at a quarter of its value.

53

After his enthronement as the first black Anglican Archbishop of Cape Town, Desmond and Leah Tutu moved out of Soweto into the luxurious Archbishop's house in Cape Town. Leah had not wanted to leave her job in Johannesburg that championed the rights of domestic servants. But she stood by Desmond as they entered the most difficult and dangerous period of their lives.

Archbishop Tutu

Then in 1986 came the news that Desmond Tutu had been elected the new Archbishop of Cape Town, the highest position in South Africa's Anglican church.

Tutu was one of the most important people in his country. He was also loved, respected, and admired throughout the world. Now he was to take on the very important job of leadership in the Anglican Church in South Africa. In his role as archbishop, he would talk on equal terms with prime ministers, monarchs, and presidents from all over the world. Yet because of the color of his skin, he was still not able to vote or hold government office in his own country. The oddity of this situation did not escape him or the rest of the world, which watched as he assumed his new role.

Desmond's enthronement, as the ceremony to install an archbishop is called, was an inspiring event for all who witnessed it. It was an even more distinguished event than the Nobel Prize ceremony had been. There was joyous singing, dancing, and prayer. Desmond invited many world leaders and celebrities to the ceremony. Among those who attended were Winnie Mandela and Coretta Scott King, widow of the great US civil rights leader, Martin Luther King, Jr.; Tutu had often been compared to King. Others who were invited to the event were politicians like US Senator Edward Kennedy, sports stars like tennis player Arthur Ashe, and pop stars like Lionel Richie and Stevie Wonder. Even such a wonderful event was marred by racism, however. The South African government would not allow all those who had been invited to enter the country.

That day, Blacks and Whites mingled in the congregation in Cape Town's great St. George's Cathedral. "How I pray that Our Lord would open our eyes so that we would see the real, the true identity of each one of us, that this is not a so-called 'Coloured,' or White, or Black or Indian, but a brother, a sister — and treat each other as such," said Desmond in a voice ringing with emotion and hope.

Tutu's enthronement was a spark of light in a land that was becoming increasingly gloomy. But it was to be only a brief spark. More political turmoil was to affect the lives of all South Africans.

"The Daily Dispatch used the occasion [of Tutu's being named Archbishop] to point out that the apartheid system had been shown to be 'no barrier to his progress.'"
Shirley du Boulay, from
Tutu: Voice of the
Voiceless

". . . reconciliation is no easy option, nor does it rule out confrontation. After all, it did cost God the death of His Son to effect reconciliation; the cross of Jesus was to expose the sinfulness of sin when He took on the powers of evil and routed them comprehensively. No, just as there can be no cheap grace so there can be no cheap reconciliation . . . we cannot cry, 'peace, peace' where there is no peace."
Desmond Tutu,
Politics and Religion — The
Seamless Garment

"At his age, [one would think Tutu] should hate a little bit more. [But] he believes in the Gospel literally."
Buti Thiagale, a Roman
Catholic priest active in the
Black Consciousness
Movement

55

Archbishop first

Now Archbishop Tutu's religious discipline became even more important to him. He remarked about the role of prayer in his life, saying the hours spent somehow "recharged my batteries."

"If I do not spend a reasonable amount of time in meditation early in the morning, then I feel a physical discomfort," he once explained. "It is worse than having forgotten to brush my teeth!"

He had always started several hours of prayer at four in the morning, then jogged for half an hour. But soon after becoming Archbishop of Cape Town, he began to have trouble with his ankle, so he had to take a brisk walk each morning instead. Breakfast, as usual, was a simple glass of fruit juice.

The days were spent receiving foreign visitors, giving press interviews, and mostly giving advice and counsel to his bishops and priests. As Archbishop he felt his role as a church leader was his main responsibility: his religion came first.

Several breaks for prayers, lunch, and a short afternoon nap filled his day. His highly disciplined routine was a habit of over twenty years as a priest. He saw it as central to his life.

For relaxation he enjoyed listening to classical music and reading religious or political books. Time spent with Leah became increasingly precious.

Whereas before the newspaper headlines had concentrated only on Tutu's punchy political statements, they now focused on his life as Archbishop. The deeply religious side of Tutu came as a surprise to many people outside the church.

Many South Africans had condemned his appointment, seeing it as political. Few knew of Tutu's academic brilliance or his deep spiritual commitment. But fellow bishops knew that Tutu would have been a prime candidate for Archbishop even if he'd never made a political speech in his life.

Tutu's political leadership was now going to prove absolutely central in the days that followed. New laws that banned all remaining anti-apartheid groups now came into force, leaving the churches as the only real opposition. Tutu's voice and leadership were now vital for the survival of the anti-apartheid movement.

The darkest days

The government, which had lifted the state of emergency, reimposed it in an even more drastic form than before. The police and army were given almost unlimited power to imprison, torture, and kill at will. Television cameras were banned from all trouble spots. The press was savagely censored.

But among the most extreme, racist Afrikaners, an even more sinister force was coming to the fore. It was a hate-filled, neo-Nazi political party called the Afrikaner Resistance Movement, or to use its Afrikaans initials, the AWB. Its members paraded with flags that reminded many world viewers of the hated swastika paraded by the Nazis. This group demanded a return to the hard-line apartheid of Dr. Verwoerd, and actually condemned P. W. Botha for being too liberal! To appease these frightening fanatics, President Botha banned peaceful opposition groups in 1988.

"We shall be free!"

Yet after so many decades of injustice and despite all the continuing cruelty and bloodshed, the pressure on white South Africans to give up their supremacy grows irresistibly. It is no longer a question of whether the system of apartheid will be dismantled. The only real question now is, "How long will these long-needed changes in policy take?"

They could take many years. Many experts predict that the powerful state and its army can keep the opposition down for decades. Others fear there may be terrible bloodshed and civil war before apartheid dies. The crackdown of 1988 made the end of this injustice seem farther away than ever.

But history is full of tyrannies that have crumbled and fallen. Archbishop Tutu and the millions of other South Africans of all colors who share his dream are certain the nightmare *must* finally come to an end.

As Tutu has put it: "Many more will be detained. Many more will be banned. Many more will be deported and killed. Yes, it will be costly. But we shall be free. Nothing will stop us from becoming free — no police bullets, dogs, tear gas, prison, death, no, nothing will stop us because God is on our side."

Right-wing backlash: Top: Neo-Nazis such as AWB leader Eugene Terre Blanche are gaining influence. Bottom: No matter much these children and their parents resist change, change is coming through the natural forces at work in South African society.

Left: Prosperous workers in the streets of modern South Africa. Many Blacks now have managerial jobs, even in senior management. The economy needs their skills. Below: Marriage between Blacks and Whites is once again allowed by the state. Tutu always stresses that individual people of different races generally get along well together. The challenge will be to sustain good will in the move to real equality and freedom.

African Anthem

Nkosi Sikele' iAfrika
God bless Africa
Maluphakanisw' uponso lwayo
Raise up her spirit
Yizwa imitandazo yetu
Hear our prayers
Usi — sikelele
And bless us

Sikelel' amadol' asizwe
Bless the leaders
Sikelela kwa nomlisela
Bless also the young
Ulitwal' ilizwe ngomonde
That they may carry the land with patience
Uwusikilele
And that you may bless them

Sikelel' amalinga etu
Bless our efforts
Awonanyana nokuzaka
To unite and lift ourselves up
Awemfundo nemvisiswano
Through learning and understanding
Uwasikelele
And bless them

Woza Moya! [Yihla] Moya!
Come Spirit! [Descend] Spirit!
Woza Moya Oyingcwele!
Come, Holy Spirit!

For More Information . . .

Organizations

The organizations listed below may provide you with more information about apartheid and about the black experience in North America, in African nations other than South Africa, and in other parts of the world. When you write, be sure to explain what you want to know and remember to include your name, address, and age.

African National Congress of South Africa
801 Second Avenue
Suite 405
New York, NY 10017

Pan-Africanist Congress
c/o United Nations
211 East 43rd Street
New York, NY 10017

Southwest Africa Peoples' Organization
801 Second Avenue
Suite 1401
New York, NY 10017

American Committee on Africa
198 Broadway
Suite 402
New York, NY 10038

Trans-Africa Forum
545 Eighth Street SE
Washington, DC 20003

Washington Office on Africa
110 Maryland Avenue NE
Washington, DC 20002

International Defense and Aid Fund
   for Southern Africa
P.O. Box 17
Cambridge, MA 02138

National Association for the Advancement
   of Colored People (NAACP)
186 Remsen Street
Brooklyn, NY 11201

United Nations Center Against Apartheid
211 East 43rd Street
New York, NY 10017

Amnesty International
322 Eighth Avenue
New York, NY 10001

World Peace Foundation of Boston
22 Batterymarch Street
Boston, MA 02109

Africa News
P.O. Box 3851
Durham, NC 27702

Groups with special programs for children —

Washington Office on Africa
110 Maryland Avenue NE
Washington, DC 20002

Lutheran World Ministries
360 Park Avenue South
New York, NY 10010

United Nations Children's Fund (UNICEF)
211 East 43rd Street
New York, NY 10017

Save the Children Federation
54 Wilton Road
Westport, CT 06880

Books

About Tutu—

Tutu, Voice of the Voiceless. du Boulay (Hodder & Stoughton)

By Tutu—
Crying in the Wilderness. (Mowbray)
Hope and Suffering. (Eerdmans)

About South Africa, apartheid, and human rights issues —

Africa. Mathabane (Macmillan)
The Apartheid Reader. McCuen (Gary E. McCuen Publications)
The Boy Child is Dying: A South African Experience. Boppell Peace (Harper & Row)
The Church Struggle in South Africa. DeGruchy (Eerdmans)
Divide and Rule: South Africa's Bantustans. Rogers (International Defense Aid Fund)
Every Kid's Guide to Understanding Human Rights. Berry (Childrens Press)
Kaffir Boy: The True Story of a Black Youth's Coming of Age in Apartheid South Africa. Mathabane (Macmillan)
Magubane's South Africa. Magubane (Knopf)
Part of My Soul Went With Him. Mandela (Norton)
South African People. Barrow (Macdonald, S.A.)
Steven Biko: Black Consciousness in South Africa. Biko (Random House)
The Struggle is My Life. Mandela (International Defense Aid Fund)
A Window on Soweto. Sikakane (International Defense Aid Fund)
You Can't Do That to Me! Famous Fights for Human Rights. Archer (Macmillan)

Glossary

African National Congress (ANC)
Founded in 1912, following the inspiration of Gandhi, to campaign for national unity and black rights. The ANC followed a policy of nonviolence until March 1960 when it was banned by the government. Today it is the main source of armed opposition from outside South Africa.

Afrikaans
The language based on a mixture of French, Dutch, and German, invented and spoken by the Boers, the original white inhabitants of South Africa.

Afrikaner Weerstands-beweging (AWB)
An extreme right-wing party that opposes democratic rule by parliament and any form of concessions to nonwhites. It has been influenced by the Nazis.

Apartheid
Literally means "apart-hood," a condition in which the races are kept apart through national laws. In the Republic of South Africa it is apartheid that promotes and maintains white dominance over Blacks in every aspect of life.

Archbishop

The highest rank of bishop, who has authority over a diocese plus those of other bishops within an area. As Archbishop of Cape Town, Tutu has all of southern Africa (including Lesotho, Swaziland, and Namibia) as his area.

Banning

The practice of prohibiting, by official decree, the free association of people and organizations who oppose the South African government's policies of apartheid. Winnie Mandela is a banned person. She may not leave her house and yard, or she will be arrested.

Bantustans

The so-called "independent" black "homelands" to which all nonwhite South Africans were forced to move, basically depriving Blacks of citizenship in their own country. The poor land that they moved to provided no income, and Blacks became impoverished. The system of removals was harsh and disruptive. Many people lost track of their loved ones.

"Black Consciousness"

A peaceful opposition movement founded and led by black political activist Steven Biko, which encouraged Blacks to be proud of their history and culture and to reject the image of Blacks as inferior to Whites.

Boer War

The war that took place from 1899 to 1902 between the Boers and the newly arrived British over control of vast South African gold fields.

Boers

Descendants of the orginal French, Dutch, and German colonists of South Africa who were mainly farmers. Also called "Afrikaners."

Censorship

The practice of removing any information considered dangerous, secret, or improper from the mail, the media (including the press), or any other form of communication. For instance, the South African government restricts press coverage of black protest. This censorship policy affects what anyone is able to learn about events and conditions there. By suppressing information, the government keeps its total power by limiting criticism by outsiders.

"Coloured"

An intermediate "racial" grouping between Bantu and White. In official language, it is used to describe people who have parents of two races.

Discrimination

Acting on an irrational hatred of a person or group based on race, sex, religion, or other attributes. The practice of racial, sexual, or religious prejudice. Denying Blacks the same quality of education as Whites is an act of racial discrimination.

Group Areas Act
The basic legislation, passed in 1950, that defines where people can live and work according to their color classification.

Kaffir
An Arabic insult dating from the nineteenth century that literally means "infidel," or nonbeliever. It is also used by Whites to insult Blacks in South Africa. The word is a racial slur, much like the US slang insult "nigger."

Komotso
"Comforter of the afflicted," a name applied to Desmond Tutu's mother, Aletha, because she was so kind and gentle.

Nazis
Members of the National Socialist German Workers' Party, which was founded in Germany in 1919 and achieved formidable power under Adolf Hitler in 1933. Nazis were a fanatical, fascist group that sought world domination and white "racial purity." They put to death millions of innocent people, six million of them Jews. This event is known as the Holocaust. The Nazi invasion of several European nations resulted in World War II (1939-45).

"Nkosi Sikele' iAfrika"
Literally meaning "God Bless Africa," it is the African anti-apartheid anthem.

Nobel Prizes
Prizes instituted in 1901 in memory of Alfred Nobel, the inventor of dynamite. They are awarded annually to people the Nobel Committee believes have made outstanding achievements in medicine, chemistry, physics, literature, economics, and peace.

Poqo
Literally meaning "standing alone," it was the military wing of an opposition group, the Pan-Africanist Congress.

Principles of nonviolence
The social philosophy that rejects any use of violence to achieve political or religious reform and instead embraces passive methods of resistance. The peaceful marches and hymn-singings that Desmond Tutu takes part in are examples of passive resistance.

Racism
The notion that one's own race or ethnic group is superior to other races. Apartheid is a way of life based on racism.

Sanctions
Penalties imposed by nations that want to apply moral or physical pressure on other nations in order to change laws or behavior. So far, economic sanctions against South Africa have not ended apartheid. The government has lifted only minor restrictions.

Segregation
  The practice of social, economic, or other separation of races, such as in housing, schools, and jobs. The South African government's forced removal of Blacks from their homes to poor urban slums is an example of segregation.

Umkhonto we Sizwe
  Literally meaning "spear of the nation," it was the military wing of the African National Congress set up by opposition leader Nelson Mandela. The movement was crushed after the arrest and life imprisonment of Mandela in 1962.

United Democratic Front (UDF)
  Founded in 1983 as an umbrella for hundreds of anti-apartheid groups across South Africa. Its goal was a nonracial South Africa achieved by nonviolence. It was banned in 1986 when the white government proclaimed a state of emergency.

Voortrekkers
  The first Boer pioneers who settled uncolonized black South African interior lands.

Chronology

1652	The Dutch East India Company settles the first Whites at Cape Town.
1795	Great Britain takes over the Cape Colony.
1809	The Hottentot Code requires every Black to live in "a fixed place."
1833	British rulers demand that the Boers free their slaves.
1837	Thousands of Afrikaners begin the Great Trek north.
1852-54	The Transvaal Republic and Orange Free State receive independence from Britain.
1866	The first diamonds are found at Kimberley, South Africa.
1877	Britain reannexes the Transvaal.
1899-1902	The British fight and win the Boer War. Thousands of Boers die in British concentration camps.
1910	The Union of South Africa is formed out of Boer and British territories. Blacks are excluded from the nation-building process.
1912	The African National Congress (ANC) is founded based on the principles of nonviolent change in an effort to regain black rights.
1931	**October 7** — Desmond Mpilo Tutu is born at Klerksdorp, 120 miles (193 km) from Johannesburg.

1936	Blacks' right to vote is abolished.
1947	Tutu is hospitalized with tuberculosis and becomes friends with Father Trevor Huddleston.
1948	The National Party wins the general election on an apartheid platform. The Group Areas Act and Population Registration Act are passed, beginning "grand apartheid."
1952	The ANC's Defiance Campaign raises its membership from seven thousand to 100 thousand. The government begins issuing Banning Orders.
1954	Tutu receives his teacher's diploma.
1955	The Bantu Education Act is passed, outlawing math and science instruction to Blacks. **July 2** — Desmond Tutu marries Leah Nomalizo Shenxane.
1956-61	The government arrests 156 ANC members and tries them for treason, but they are eventually acquitted.
1958	Tutu enters St. Peter's Theological College to begin religious training.
1959	Eight Bantustans, or "homelands," are set up by the government. Millions of Blacks are forced from their homes to live in distant areas.
1960	British Prime Minister Harold Macmillan delivers his "Wind of Change" speech to the South African Parliament. **March 21** — The Pan-Africanist Congress (PAC) assembles five thousand Blacks in the Sharpeville township to protest peacefully against Pass Laws. Police open fire into the crowd, killing sixty-nine and wounding 180. Tutu is ordained a deacon in the Anglican Church.
1961	Nelson Mandela forms *Umkhonto we Sizwe*, a military wing of the ANC, to sabotage government targets. Tutu is ordained a priest.
1962	Nelson Mandela is arrested and later sentenced to life in prison. **September** — Tutu goes to London to study theology at King's College.
1963	The International Olympic Committee demands that South Africa desegregate its team before an invitation to participate in the 1964 Olympic Games will be issued.
1968	Tutu returns to South Africa to teach at St. Peter's College, Alice. While there, Black students are brutalized by police during a peaceful demonstration. The incident is a turning point for Tutu. The Black Consciousness movement is founded by Steven Biko.

1970	Tutu begins his duties as lecturer at the University of Botswana, Lesotho, and Swaziland.
1972	Tutu becomes Associate Director of the Theological Education Fund in London, England.
1975	Tutu becomes Dean of Johannesburg. The Minister of Bantu Education decrees that arithmetic and social studies may be taught in black schools, but only in the Afrikaans language.
1976	Tutu writes to Prime Minister Vorster warning of the violence that will happen if oppression continues. **June 16** — A peaceful demonstration by black schoolchildren in Soweto is fired on by police. Rioting erupts in black townships in protest. **July** — Tutu is consecrated Bishop of Lesotho.
1977	**September 12** — Steven Biko dies in police custody. World protest erupts against apartheid. Tutu delivers the funeral oration.
1978	Tutu becomes General Secretary of the South African Council of Churches. P.W. Botha becomes Prime Minister.
1979	Tutu calls for economic sanctions against the South African government on Danish television.
1983	Prime Minister Botha calls for a referendum on a new parliament that will include Whites, "Indians," and "Coloureds," but not Blacks. Only Whites may vote on it.
1984	Blacks begin killing other Blacks for suspected collaboration with their white oppressors. **December** — Tutu receives the Nobel Peace Prize in Oslo, Norway.
1985	**February 3** — Tutu is enthroned as Bishop of Johannesburg.
1986	**April** — Tutu is elected Archbishop of Cape Town, head of the Anglican Church in South Africa. **June** — P.W. Botha, president under the new constitution, declares a state of emergency to deal with black unrest.
1988	Botha bans all remaining anti-apartheid groups to appease neo-Nazi groups. Police are given unlimited powers of arrest. **August** — The Trade Union Building in Johannesburg, headquarters of Tutu and anti-apartheid groups, is destroyed by a bomb.

Index